Building New Wealth

Building New Worlds

A Nine-Month Program
for the Absolute Beginner

Edward Pittman

SIRIUS INK

www.siriusink.com

First edition published by
Sirius Productions
Wilsonville, OR 97070
USA

ISBN: 978-0-9847767-2-6

Book Layout & Pre-Press:
Philip H. Farber
http://www.hawkridgeproductions.com

Cover Design:
Fergal Fitzpatrick
http://www.fergalfitzpatrick.com

"Making money is art and working is art and good business is the best art." - Andy Warhol

CONTENTS

BUILDING NEW WEALTH, BUILDING NEW WORLDS

Nothing is more "bottom line" than money - after all, financial statements are where the expression "bottom line" comes from. It has been a key, everyday factor in the survival and existence of nearly every man, woman and child on this planet for thousands of years.

It is rather strange, then, that so many people today view money and its workings as either a mystery or hold gross misunderstandings about the whole subject. Being largely cut off from real financial understanding, they make do with less prosperity than they might otherwise enjoy - perhaps much less.

This course is written for the absolute beginner when it comes to understanding money and the building of wealth. However, it contains perspectives and ideas that may also be new and inspiring to more seasoned wealth-builders. The lessons promote three factors as being necessary in this endeavor: Economic Understanding, Wealth Psychology and Personal Finance Tools. Combining these essential factors, the course serves as a common gateway that everyone can pass through and emerge well-equipped to travel further in the wealth-building directions most suitable for them. (Further resources are listed as Appendix Two.)

The lessons are meant to be worked through over a period of nine months, taken one lesson per month. If you want to work more slowly, you should still keep definite deadlines for passing from one lesson to the next so as to keep yourself moving. It is not recommended that you work more quickly than one lesson per month as keeping the ideas and themes of the lessons within your awareness for an extended period of time is an important part of how the course works.

Each lesson ends with a section called "Taking Action" that lists several things for you to do in building wealth that month in connection with the themes of the particular lesson. Even the lessons that may seem more abstract or philosophical are very action-oriented. This is because these actions are not just about creating outer changes but also for fully internalizing what is learned.

The aim of this course is to help Individual people to become more wealthy, especially those people that might not have ever dreamed that greater prosperity was possible for them. That is the "hook" that you care about and which has you reading. But the greater purpose behind this course is much wider in scope and is right there in the title: Building New Wealth and Building New Worlds. As more and more Individuals (a) become wise in the ways of money and wealth, and (b) begin to create more wealth for themselves and new forms of wealth in society, new worlds will indeed blossom.

LESSON ONE:
INTRODUCTION TO MONEY

This lesson, being the first, is intended to provide you with a basic orientation. When you have read it and completed its actions, you will have knowledge concerning the basic factors involved in building wealth, the history and evolution of money, some facts about your money, your management of it and what immediate activities might begin to improve your financial reality. That is what you are doing in this lesson, beginning to clearly establish your financial reality by bringing these things into clear focus.

Even if you knew some of these things before, your attention will be put back upon them. You may learn new things. In any case, you will begin to establish a basic reality of wealth-building that will be gradually expanded and deepened by the lessons that follow.

THREE FACTORS IN BUILDING WEALTH

In building wealth, there are three essential factors to consider. Unfortunately, many people today are lacking - and even damaged - in all three areas of wealth competence. This is why so many people, including entire nations, have problems with money. These three factors are as follows:

PERSONAL FINANCE TOOLS are needed for tracking your money, saving it, investing it and protecting it. When people in an affluent society with a relatively free market have problems with money, one of the main reasons might simply be that their financial affairs need to be better organized.

WEALTH PSYCHOLOGY addresses and cultivates the beliefs and attitudes that help you to have a good relationship with money, to create wealth, to maintain wealth and to fully enjoy the wealth that you possess. In fact, as these lessons progress, you will come to understand the building of wealth as a method of overall personal growth.

ECONOMIC UNDERSTANDING, particularly of the essential natures of money and the General Market, provides the fundamental context of your activity. The desire for more money is the initial motivation for most people that want to build wealth. The General Market is the environment in which wealth is created. It is therefore fundamentally important to understand these things and how they work.

One of the main reasons that these lessons were written is that most books, courses or other materials usually focus on only one or two of these factors. All three are necessary. This course aims to guide you in cultivating all three factors so that your new reality of wealth will be more complete, balanced and stable. Moreover, by following this approach, you will then be able to go ahead and use those other, more specialized resources more effectively because you will better understand where, how and why they fit into your bigger picture. A list of such resources is included in Appendix Two for further research after completing these lessons.

You might think of these three elements as being similar to the elements needed to make fire. To have fire, you need to have fuel, oxygen and heat. Having one or even two of these things will not give you fire. You must have all three. Once you have fire, you can then have light, warmth, cooking, metallurgy, steam and gasoline engines, even rocket ships, as well as a lot of other things along the way. First, though, you need that initial reaction that produces fire. As the presence of fuel, oxygen and heat can result in the ignition of fire, so can the combination of Personal Finance Tools, Wealth Psychology and Economic Understanding ignite the energizing "fire" of wealth in your life. As the mastery of fire has allowed humanity to create increasingly sophisticated technology, so can the mastery of this wealth "fire" allow you to create an increasingly fulfilling and wealthy existence.

THE HISTORY AND EVOLUTION OF MONEY

We will begin by starting to get to know money as a thing in itself, by looking at its history and seeing what it is and how it came into being.

Within an immediate kinship group, there is a basic division of labor and members of the group voluntarily give portions of the fruits of their labor to other members. This is what is known as a "gift economy" and still persists within family households in essentially the same way that it functioned in early human groups. As trade expands among larger groups without immediate kinship affinity and involving more advanced goods and services, barter emerges as the form of exchange. Barter is also a direct exchange of goods and services without the use of money, but is more formal and balanced than gifting. The larger, more complex and more sophisticated webs of exchange facilitated by barter provide the platform for the development of culture and civilization.

Even in our modern society, barter can still be very useful and will always have its place, but it exhibits a number of serious problems as a large-scale system. The most immediate problem is in matching up the needs and wants of the participants. Unless the society is quite primitive, with very few skills and goods in its market, it may become quite complicated to always find people that have what you want but also want what you have. This would be impossible in our society where goods and services are so diversified to cater to such a wide variety of specialized, personal needs and tastes. We all want what the farmer provides, but he does not necessarily want everything that we provide.

Another issue is the indivisibility of certain goods.

Suppose now that you are the farmer and need a variety of goods and services provided by a blacksmith, a physician and a tailor. Perhaps, due to the season or a poor harvest, you only have a horse or plow for exchange. Obviously, you can not break up the horse or plow and divide it among the three places where you need to trade. Again, if this is a problem in commercially simple cultures, just imagine the difficulties there would be in our much more complex one.

So, to facilitate trade, basic commodities such as grain, salt or oil emerge as mediums of exchange. Here, we see the basic forms of money. Alternatively, some primitive forms of money included objects that were simply rare and difficult to obtain, such as the eyeteeth of certain animals or special kinds of shells. Money, as a medium of exchange, resolves the problems of barter and provides another tremendous boost to the further advancement of economic culture. When exchanges are made in money, the exchange ratios of all goods and services can be quantified and compared in the language of specific *prices*. This allows farmers, craftsmen, merchants and all other businessmen to calculate their expenses and profits, which facilitates the formation of an elaborate structure of production.

In money, then, we have something that acts as a store of value, as a medium for exchanging value and as a quantitative unit of account.

Historically and globally, many commodities have

served but precious metals have emerged as the most popular forms of money. They possess several properties that make this so. Gold and silver are both rare and durable. In these properties, they provide a more stable money supply than things like grain that are perishable or variable in quantity. They also have a property known as "fungibility" which means that one unit of the commodity is equivalent in quality to any other unit. One measure of pure metal is equivalent to another. A contrasting example would be precious gems, which are also rare and durable but lack this fungibility because individual gems have different characteristics.

With the emergence of precious metals as money, the invention of coins was a logical development. Coins permit the exchange of metal in small units of standardized weight, greatly facilitating everyday commerce. Using the examples from above, coins combine the commodity value of a sack of a grain with the portability and durability of rare shells or animal teeth. Coins appear to have emerged nearly 3000 years ago, though there is disagreement as to whether they were first used in India, Greece or Anatolia (Turkey). Up until very recently, coins have been the most commonly used forms of money in everyday exchange and are archetypal symbols of money.

For merchants and wholesalers involved in large transactions, however, it becomes tiresome to be continually moving around large amounts of metal. It is much more convenient to warehouse one's money and trade receipts of deposit. In this, we have the origins of banking and banknotes. Banknotes were first used in ancient China and appeared in Europe during the late medieval period. Originally, these privately-issued notes could be redeemed for the amount of precious metal for which they were an actual receipt. Today, however, currencies are issued by state treasuries and central banks, with their value determined by law, and are not directly representative of precious metals or any other commodity. This is known as "fiat" money from the Latin term for a decree. The governments and central banks simply decree that the currency has value.

This represents a substantive change in the nature of money and how people think of it. You will remember from above that it was the gold or silver substance of a coin that constituted "money" and we can describe the coin, in form, as merely the packaging of that commodity. Over time, this distinction has become blurred and even reversed - abetted by the further abstraction of the warehouse receipts and their development into paper currency - until today, we have currencies that derive their value solely from the political authority of their issuers. Moreover, these issuers can increase the total supply of currency in circulation at will by simply printing more, resulting in decreasing purchasing power. This is known as "inflation."

With worries growing about the lack of real value in modern currencies and the steady erosion of purchasing power caused by inflation, some voices have been heard calling for monetary reform. Some advise returning to the use of precious metals, others advocate currencies tied to "baskets" of multiple commodities and yet others simply want to open the marketplace to multiple forms of money and allow them to compete in the marketplace like any other commodity or product. These voices are still in the minority but are becoming louder and more widespread. We are not going to go into these issues deeply in this course, but it is important to be aware of them. In such a time of crisis and opportunity, it is especially crucial that people fully understand the nature of money and wealth.

KEEPING TRACK OF YOUR MONEY

Your primary activity for this lesson is to start tracking all of the money that you spend. This means every penny, or whatever the equivalent is in your own currency. This is not hard to do. You can carry a notebook or use a smart phone application and log the amounts as you spend the money, or you can collect receipts from transactions and log the expenditures later. You can organize the information on paper or in a computer file. Whatever method that you prefer is fine, so long as you track all of the money that is spent and what it is spent on. Make this a routine, second nature.

By doing this, you will KNOW where your money goes. You will SEE your financial life CLEARLY. Some people may have no real idea where there money goes. Others might think that they know, but could encounter some surprises. Some may actually have a good idea of how they spend their money, but will now know in full detail. All will benefit. This tracking is meant to begin introducing you to an objective perception of your financial reality. This moves you into a position of control. Later, you will use this tracking to better organize your spending. For now, though, do not judge but simply observe.

FACING UP TO YOUR MONEY ISSUES

Because money is so fundamental to survival and quality of life, it can evoke many strong feelings. Depending on factors of personality, life experience or present conditions, there may be things about money that a person does not want to face up to. This can take many forms: fear and worry, laziness and procrastination, forgetfulness and disorganization, pretense and lies, shame, blame, regrets and excuses. Do you experience any of these phenomena regarding money or financial matters?

As these phenomena accumulate, they prevent wealth from existing. So, a secondary benefit of really getting to know money - and especially your own - is that you can begin to clear out the anti-wealth muck that may have accumulated in your areas of previous ignorance and inattention. If you are willing to increase your wealth-building awareness and ability, the way to begin is:

A. Identify an aspect of money that you are not facing up to.

B. Face it, take responsibility for it and deal with it. Invest the effort and persistence required to resolve it.

To initiate this process, consider the questions below. Write out your answers. (You may wish to start a special journal for recording your work with this course.)

1. Are your accounts balanced?

2. What is your monthly income?

3. How much money do you spend per month? On what?

4. How much money do you waste per month?

5. Do you owe any money? How much?

6. How much debt interest do you pay per month?

7. Are you not paying money that you promised to pay?

8. Are you avoiding anyone who owes you money?

9. Are you involved in a financial disagreement?

10. Do you avoid preparing tax forms?

11. What are you doing with money that you should not be doing?

And finally, because you may need some cheering up at this point:

12. What are you doing right?

Depending upon your situation, the answers to these questions may leave you feeling unhappy or overwhelmed. However, you must take heart. Had you continued to ignore these issues, they would have continued to fester and plague you. Now, you can begin to handle them. As you do, each resolution will make you feel liberated and relieved, as well as opening up more space for wealth in your life. Some of these may be things that you can resolve immediately, simply by buckling down and doing so. Others may require more time. That is alright because you are just getting started and your wealth competence will increase with each lesson that follows.

TAKING ACTION

So, to conclude this lesson:

1. Start tracking your expenses and continue to do so.

2. Answer the questions above to determine any present money issues that you may have. Resolve any revealed money issues that you can now.

3. Continue to be aware of money issues to be resolved as soon as possible and do so.

NOTES

NOTES

NOTES

NOTES

LESSON TWO: YOUR DEEPER RELATIONSHIP WITH MONEY

In the previous lesson, the aim was to look at money in a concrete and objective way. This applied to both money as a thing in itself and to your own personal finances. Maybe you saw money and your handling of it in a new way. Maybe you were really looking at it for the first time. Building directly upon those initial insights, the aim in this lesson is to use what you have learned so as to better understand and appreciate money from even deeper philosophical and psychological perspectives. This will prepare you to work with money in an essentially new and powerful way.

At this time, it might be worthwhile to go back and review the section of Lesson One that explains the history and evolution of money so that it is fresh in your mind. Then, we can deepen our understanding of the role and function of money in this lesson. Please do that now and return here when you have finished.

THE PITH OF CIVILIZATION

In describing the evolution of money, we listed several qualities or factors of the kind of money that emerges under ideal conditions. While these desirable factors contribute to the soundness of money, they are secondary to the essential function of money as a medium of exchange and it is this function that remains and struggles along in even the most debased and inflated forms of money. To approach a deeper understanding of money, then, let us examine this matter of EXCHANGE.

Suppose that humans lived in total isolation from each other and only came together to mate. Imagine that every Individual was forced to build their own home, make their own clothes, hunt and grow their own food and so on. No one would have much time for anything beyond eking out a daily subsistence. Everyone's life would be roughly the same. Any clever tricks or insights that an Individual might come up with for making life easier or giving it more meaning would die with them. Indeed, even the implied carpentry, clothes-making and agriculture mentioned above would not really exist.

However, with social exchange among Individuals, people can divide various labors amongst themselves and specialize in work according to their own personal aptitude and taste. This results in greater personal expression and fulfillment, giving the life of each Individual greater personal meaning. It also makes it possible for Individuals to make more new innovations in their work so as to accomplish it with greater efficiency and effectiveness. There is also time and energy for creative arts and personal recreation. And through exchange, all of this innovation and novelty can be communicated and begins to spread. As a rising tide lifts all boats, all Individuals benefit from this process and can then continue it even further.

This is why the economist Ludwig von Mises said that Economics "is the philosophy of human life and action and concerns everybody and everything. It is the pith of civilization and of Man's human existence."

For you, personally, having more money really means having more freedom and power to do the things that you want to do. We need money to survive but it also helps us to thrive and to fully enjoy the pleasures of life. Money is a means to purchase material luxuries, of course, but it also facilitates having fun with our family and friends, learning new things, supporting causes that we care about and improving our worlds in every way.

To truly appreciate money, though, means more than just appreciating HAVING money and it means more than just appreciating YOUR money. It also means appreciating money in itself and for its role in creation. Consider the following three factors:

A. In every voluntary commercial exchange, money is given to satisfy some need, desire or aim of the spender. The recipient of the money will later use it to satisfy their own personal needs, desires or aims.

B. The sum of such exchanges comprises the

dynamic flow of social energies.

C. Money is properly a commodity, itself, in addition to being a means for exchanging other commodities.

Keeping these factors in mind, then, we can see that in money there is a meeting of purpose, energy and substance. In effect, money acts as a force of creation and transformation. So, when we talk about wealth-building, what we really mean in the ultimate sense is WORLD-building, with money as the means for building worlds and worlds-within-worlds.

FACING UP TO YOUR DEEPER MONEY ISSUES

Money reflects the dynamic motion and expansiveness inherent in social energies. These energies flow through our lives as money flows through our lives. To create wealth, these energies must flow freely and we must channel them artfully.

However, anti-money and anti-wealth attitudes, held consciously or unconsciously, will cause us to misdirect these energies. Moreover, such attitudes will choke the flows down to mere trickles or may block them off entirely.

In the previous lesson, you answered questions that were intended to expose problem areas in your handling of your money. Answering the following questions can help to expose deeper issues that you may have with money in itself.

1. What do you lie about regarding money?

2. What bad habits do you have with money?

3. What scares you about money?

4. What are you putting off?

5. What do you hate about money?

6. Looking at any problems revealed by the questions above, how did the problems originate in your life?

Write out the answers in your journal.

If you answer these questions honestly and thoroughly, you can begin to uncover whatever problem areas that you might have and can then begin to take conscious action in handling them. Awareness is key. Once you have exposed any problems and put your attention on them, you must remain alert and notice when you are acting upon them or otherwise reinforcing them. When you catch yourself acting in ways that are dictated by bad attitudes about money, you must stop and correct your behavior. Remind yourself why. Also, when you find yourself giving voice · aloud or internally · to bad attitudes about money, stop and correct yourself. If you are disciplined in this activity, you can begin to break up anti·money psychological patterns that may be preventing you from building wealth.

It may be possible, though, that you have problems with money that lurk below your conscious awareness and that are resistant to your conscious efforts at change. These attitudes may have been formed when you were very young, and may even be inherited from your parents or other people in your childhood environment. In such cases, you may need to seek out mental change technologies such as Hypnosis or Neuro-Linguistic Programming to help you in making the changes that you want. Of course, also using such technologies for subconscious reinforcement of pro-money and pro-wealth attitudes is something that can be of benefit to anyone.

APPRECIATING MONEY AND WEALTH

Meanwhile, there are several things that you can do to consciously boost your appreciation of money. One way is to consider the opposites of the questions asked above. How have you become more honest about money? What good money habits have you cultivated? What money issues have you handled? What do you like about money? Write the answers to these questions in your journal, as well, and revisit them periodically to see how your attitudes may have changed. As you continue to work on your relationship with money, your answers to these questions will expand.

Another thing to do is to be actively appreciative of

money. Whenever you receive some money, express thanks right then (even if only mentally). Likewise, whenever you SPEND money or pay bills, you should also express thanks right then for the goods or services that the money is buying for you. Whether receiving money or receiving value in exchange for money, express gratitude in the moment. Sometimes, at first, this may feel forced - especially when paying bills. Stick with it and it will become a genuine and habitual attitude.

Practice being appreciative of other people's financial success. Many people envy the rich and tell themselves that anyone who is successful must have become so unethically. Certainly, some people have become wealthy in this way. However, most people that achieve financial success have done so by providing a good or service that other people want. Appreciate and admire that when you see it. After all, these people are enjoying the kind of success that you want for yourself. You send a bad message to yourself if you ignore or disdain it. Look for this kind of success and admire it when you find it. Again, you may feel resistance here but stick with it.

Practice being appreciative and admiring of beautiful things and quality goods. This does not necessarily mean desiring them all for yourself, but simply appreciating that they exist and admiring how they enhance the world. Give your appreciation and admiration to the benefits that the sciences have produced, the quality of life that they have given to you and to humanity in general over previous generations, centuries and millenia. Look for these things and admire them when you encounter them.

By clearing out your unconscious and habitual anti-money and anti-wealth attitudes and replacing them with conscious and habitual pro-money and pro-wealth attitudes, you will deeply transform your reality as to what is possible for you and will provide a firm foundation for building wealth.

YOUR SOCIAL MATRIX

Another factor in your attitudes toward money and wealth can be found in your relationships with others. It was just pointed out that some of your attitudes may have been inherited from your parents or other people that were around you as a child. People with the same attitudes and the same general level of material success in life tend to cluster together. If you have problems with money, bad attitudes toward money and wealth, or both, you may probably have close associates that are in the same situation. More, you may be reinforcing each other to remain in the same sort of existence.

As you change, you may find yourself losing affinity with some of the people around you. You are going to notice any anti-money and anti-wealth attitudes and behaviors displayed by your intimates more clearly and will likely be somewhat put-off by them (though you should keep in mind that they were also once your attitudes and behaviors). Likewise, some of those close to you may become jealous or distrustful of the changes in you and your more prosperous lifestyle. You may naturally wish to share the information and techniques that you have used in creating these changes. Do so, as you think appropriate, but you should be aware that some people may still reject or even mock them - even with the proof of your own success right in front of them.

On the other hand, you will also probably be interested in forming new relationships with others that share your new viewpoint and growing prosperity. Just as an old social matrix can reinforce bad attitudes and behaviors that hold you down, a new social matrix can reinforce the good attitudes and behaviors that will help you to create beneficial change and to build wealth.

To assist in handling these changes, you should begin to confront these issues directly now. Ask yourself these additional questions:

What kind of attitudes do the people around me have toward money? What is their relationship with money like?

To what extent am I willing for my relationships to change as my financial situation improves? What changes might be good to make now?

By considering these issues now, you will be more prepared for them if and when they may arise.

TAKING ACTION

1. Consider: *"As a single footstep will not make a path on the earth, so a single thought will not make a pathway in the mind. To make a deep physical path, we walk again and again. To make a deep mental path, we must think over and over the kind of thoughts we wish to dominate our lives."* - Henry David Thoreau

2. Continue to think about the "History and Evolution of Money" section of Lesson One and the "Pith of Civilization" section from this lesson.

3. Face up to your deeper money issues by answering the questions asked in this lesson. Begin working on resolving them consciously while also seeking out a practitioner or products that can help you with the deeper, unconsciously-held beliefs and attitudes that you may have, as needed. Be watchful for other issues or areas of resistance that may arise as you work with the lessons to come.

4. Be mindful of opportunities to actively appreciate money and wealth as they arise. Express gratitude for your money as it comes in and for what it brings you as you pay it out. Practice appreciating and admiring the financial success of others and the more general creation of wealth in the world.

5. Be aware that your relationships may change as your wealth increases, consider in what ways you are willing for your relationships to change and think about what changes you might wish to actively make. Go ahead and make any changes

that you think are appropriate now. Note that you may be able to simply diminish certain relationships without having to completely terminate them.

6. Continue to track your spending. Continue to resolve money issues from Lesson One as needed.

NOTES

NOTES

NOTES

NOTES

LESSON THREE: ESTABLISHING YOUR FOUNDATION

Wealth is a state of abundance. It means having the freedom and resources to do what you want to do, when you want to do it and to live a life that is completely true to yourself. This state of abundance is not entirely about money, of course, but having sufficient money is certainly a crucial resource in enjoying wealth.

The first two lessons of this course focused on improving your understanding of money and your relationship with it. By doing so, you will now be better prepared for working with money and beginning to build wealth. You may even already be enjoying significant, beneficial changes in your financial affairs. Now, in this lesson, you will begin to organize your handling of your money and other resources so as to establish a reliable foundation upon which wealth may be built.

THE ESSENTIAL FORMULA

Seas of ink have been spilled on the subject of wealth and how it may be acquired. Underneath all sound explanations, there is but one essential formula. If you follow this formula, you can not help but accumulate wealth. This is so for both the poor and the rich. If you do not follow this formula, it will become impossible for you to accumulate wealth. Even if you were to inherit a fortune or win a lottery, that wealth would soon be lost if you were to disregard the truth and power of this formula.

Produce more than you consume.

That is the essential formula. In terms of money, this means keeping the level of your spending below the level of your income. The amount of money that goes out from you must be less - not equal to, and certainly not greater - than the amount of money that comes in.

However, this formula does not only apply to money. As a simple example, suppose that you have a fruit tree. If you do not eat every fruit that the tree produces, you might preserve and store the extra fruit to have in the winter. You could also trade or sell some of it to others. Either way, by not eating every fruit that the tree produces, you accumulate a surplus.

To build wealth, you must use this essential formula to produce a surplus that can grow. Of course, there are two components to this formula that can be used to make it work: you can produce more or you can consume less. Doing both will make the formula work more quickly.

In this lesson, the focus will be upon learning to *consume less*. As you can never fill a water bucket that is full of holes, you will need to master the art of conserving what you already have before you turn your attention to *producing more* in the lessons that follow.

FILLING IN THE HOLES

First and foremost, if you have debt, you MUST eliminate it as quickly as possible. Debt and the interest that it accumulates are, again, like holes in a water bucket. You will not be able to build financial wealth while they are a part of your financial life.

The most important and immediate aspect of this is to stop accumulating new debt. If you have credit cards, you must stop using them. If you feel unsafe without having the credit card for emergencies, you need to begin saving into an emergency fund. If you need to do this, it will be a part of creating your monthly spending plan as described below. Cancel all recurring payments and shopping accounts tied to your card(s) NOW, then destroy the actual cards just as soon as your emergency fund is equal to your credit limit.

When your emergency fund is ready, begin paying off your debts. If you have multiple debts, you might consider paying them off in order from smallest to largest. By doing so, the number of debts diminishes more quickly. Those who recommend this method claim to experience a psychological satisfaction in seeing this happen that helps them to sustain momentum in paying the debts off completely.

MAKING A PLAN

You have been tracking your spending for a couple of months now, so you have probably already started to think about budgeting to some degree. You have probably already seen some ways to beneficially change your spending habits, even if you have not yet considered a comprehensive plan. In any case, now is the time to really focus on making that plan.

Budgets are like diets. There are many different types, all with their own books and advocates. They all seem to work for some people while failing miserably for others. That is because people are DIFFERENT and have different needs, tastes and lifestyles. The key to creating a successful budget - one that you will stick with - is to create a system that adheres to the essential formula of producing more than you consume while still satisfying your personal needs, tastes and lifestyle. Tracking your spending over the past two months will have helped prepare you for creating such a system.

Also like dieting, many people dread living by a budget because they believe that it will be horribly oppressive. You may feel like the budget would be a cruel and austere Master that you must serve slavishly. On the contrary, though, a well-made plan crafted to suit your needs and goals will be your faithful servant and will provide you with wealth. So, we will use the term "spending plan" rather than the word "budget" from now on. This is not just a euphemism to gloss over the unpleasant associations of budgeting, though that is a benefit. It is actually a more appropriate and descriptive term for what you will be doing - spending according to a PLAN designed to produce financial wealth.

A basic spending plan is offered below. Try it on and see how it fits. If your financial situation is desperate and you find that you just can not use this plan, you might follow it as best you can and use it as a goal to work toward. Its structure is merely a suggestion, though you may find it to be a good one as you continue to work through this course.

Again, you have been tracking your spending for a couple of months now and have probably already seen where some changes can be made. Take that knowledge and implement this spending plan by allocating your money as follows:

50% to NEEDS (such as housing, food, transportation and necessary clothing)

20% to WANTS (such as entertainment, restaurant meals and nights out, extra clothing)

10% to SAVINGS and INVESTMENT

10% to DEEP INDULGENCE

10% to TITHING

You may have experienced some alarm and confusion at these percentages, being asked to live on only 70% of your income and to commit 20% of your income to strange categories. If you are having trouble making ends meet now, this plan may seem impossible. You may be unfamiliar with tithing and almost certainly wonder what we mean by "Deep Indulgence." Please keep reading and hear us out.

First, let us address the issue of tithing. Tithing is a practice usually associated with religious groups, in which adherents give the first 10% of their incomes to their church or equivalent body. This is the financial equivalent of sacrificing the "first fruits" of labor in gratitude and to consecrate the material wealth that is offered to the spiritual source that is central to the lives of the tithers.

However, if you are not religious, there are still things that recommend tithing as a valuable practice. First, to give away the first 10% of your income puts you in a state of abundance, psychologically. If you can give away some of your money before you have even spent any on yourself, and you see that your world does not end, you are certainly going to feel wealthy. Second, regularly giving money to an organization that supports your highest values is going to consecrate (make sacred) your wealth to you, in your own mind. If you have money issues of the type covered in the previous lesson, tithing will help you to feel justified in your wealth and more deserving of it.

These two reasons are not just tricks to make you feel good, though. You will feel good because you are actually doing something good. You are creating something real. Moreover, your giving will probably be tax deductible! So, if traditional church tithing is not for you, you might pay your tithe to a fraternal organization, school or scholarship fund, museum or whatever reflects your own highest values.

Deep Indulgence is spending money on things that make you happy. In other spending plans, these things might be included among "Wants", but Deep Indulgence is something more than the smaller, everyday indulgences that belong in that category. Deep Indulgence is experienced through the Big Things that satisfy your deeper dreams and desires. This course is just as much about your growth as an Individual as it is about growing your wealth - and the relationship between the two - so Deep Indulgence is separated into its own category to make sure that it happens. This subject will be covered in much more detail in next month's lesson. For now, just hold on to this money while keeping it separate from your regular savings.

If you use credit cards, your savings might first go toward establishing a basic emergency fund that is equal to your credit limit. Once this has been done, your savings should go toward paying off the cards and any other debt that you may have. When your debt has been paid off, savings should be directed back to the emergency fund. Otherwise, you may just start on an emergency fund immediately if you do not have debts to handle. The emergency fund should eventually be equal to at least three months of your income, but six months is better. Some people even build year-sized emergency funds.

This money is only to be used in actual emergencies, to help cope with the unexpected and catastrophic financial blows that can occur in life. When your emergency fund is in place, you can then start looking at investment and retirement saving. Again, this will be covered in more detail in a future lesson.

THRIFT AND FRUGAL LIVING

Within the structure of your spending plan, you can

begin cutting down on the money that you spend on both needs and wants by embracing the virtue of thrift.

Thrift can mean different things to different people, widely ranging from skipping expensive coffee drinks and clipping a few coupons to pursuing total Self-sufficiency in a mountain cabin. You find the level that works best for you and supports your needs and desires. Thrift or frugal living is not about depriving yourself or being a miser, it is about getting the most for your money. The word "thrift" is related to the word "thrive" and the word "frugal" derives from the Latin word for fruits. So, far from being a bleak and joyless lifestyle, frugal living can help to provide you with increasing security and ultimately more luxury than spending thoughtlessly.

Thrift begins with prioritizing your spending. Evaluate your expenses and any purchases that you might be considering. You can first prioritize them by their necessity - whether they are life-sustaining, important or a luxury. You can then prioritize them by time - whether they are needed or wanted now or can wait for the future. You can do this with lists and can also work on making it a habitual way of thinking.

In addition to prioritizing your needs and wants, you will want to learn how to find the best deals on new things, how to make old things last longer and function better and how to easily make things for yourself that you would normally buy. There are all kinds of books, magazines, web sites and groups that share tools, tricks and secrets for saving money on practically everything. You might also enjoy coming up with new ways on your own.

If you have a family, you should get everyone involved in the frugal living process. Your household thrift may be thought of quite literally and seriously as a "Family Business."

WHAT YOU HAVE NOW

In the first lesson, you were asked to look objectively at your habits in handling money. In this lesson, now, you will calculate your net worth as an objective standard of your financial wealth. Rather than looking to increase income alone, without regard to debt or other factors, it makes sense to measure financial wealth by what you actually HAVE.

To calculate your net worth, begin by adding up the value of your home (if you own it), any other real estate that you might own and your vehicle(s). Determine the current value of these things, not what you paid for them. Next, add up the amount of money that you hold in savings, checking and retirement accounts, certificates of deposit or cash.

Finally, add up the value of other tangible assets that you own such as electronics, furniture, jewelry, collectible coins or bullion, art or antiques and so on. Include anything with a value of over $500 (or the equivalent in your currency), but be conservative in your estimates. Combine these three values together and that is the total value of your assets.

Now, total up any debts that you have (mortgage or other loans, credit cards and so on) and subtract that amount from the total value of your assets. The total value of your assets minus the total of your liabilities is your net worth.

This number may be big, it may be small or it may even be negative. Whatever the case, you now have it as something objective to look at and measure as your actions make it change. By following the essential formula - producing more than you consume - you can begin to make it grow and you can objectively see it grow as it happens. What is really great about this is that you do not even need more money to start making your net worth grow right now. By using the information in this lesson, you can start this growth immediately by just making better use of what you already have.

However, you also have a lot of additional wealth that is not calculated in your net worth. You may not even be used to thinking of these resources as "wealth" because they are not immediately related to money or luxury goods - but they may be used to acquire money, luxury goods or anything else that you want out of life.

These resources include things like your senses and physical capabilities, your time and its management, your intelligence and creativity, your personal knowledge and experience, your level of education, employment skills, hobby skills, tools and equipment, books, public libraries, telephone(s), computers and their software, all of the information and communication resources of the internet and many, many other things in addition to the material resources that make up your net worth. Moreover, if you have good relationships and some ability in influencing others, then you may have some access to the resources of the people around you.

You have certain resources available to you. You can gain the cooperation of others in the use of their resources. Not only can you use those resources in creating the life that you want, but you can use them to obtain or control MORE, NEW resources. You have the ability to utilize all of these resources to create practically anything that you want, and you have the ability to expand your creations virtually without limit and in all directions. Cultivate the habit of constantly looking for additional resources that you can utilize.

Know that manifesting your goals is a process that, however ambitious, can be achieved by organizing the work into doable steps. Gather and coordinate progressively more and more resources to take ever bigger and more powerful steps.

TAKING ACTION

1. As you work through this lesson, continue to be aware of any resistances or psychological issues of the kind described in the previous lesson that may come up. Handle them as advised in Lesson Two.

2. If you have debt, begin paying it down immediately. Be sure not to accumulate new debt.

3. Create and implement a spending plan. If you wish, experiment with it and adjust the percentages until you find what is optimal for you - but only adjust the savings percentage UPWARD. Continue tracking your spending, of course.

4. Adopt the mindset of thrift and incorporate it into your lifestyle. Look for books, magazines, web sites and groups that provide ideas and tips for saving money and frugal living. Begin implementing whatever practices are suitable for the lifestyle that you truly want to create.

5. Calculate your net worth and establish it as an objective standard of your financial wealth and as a target of increase. Recalculate it periodically, perhaps monthly as you work with this course and then quarterly from then on.

6. Think about all of the extra-financial resources that you possess or have access to that can help you

in building wealth. Create an exhaustive list of these resources in your journal and look for ways to put them to use as you work through this entire course. Update the list regularly and continue to use this meta-resource for the rest of your life. Your resourcefulness should become a strong component of your character and you will learn to apply it in all areas of your existence.

NOTES

NOTES

NOTES

NOTES

LESSON FOUR: BUYING HAPPINESS

It is often said that money can not buy happiness. A common retort to people who say this is that they just do not know where to shop. There is truth in both statements. If we think of money as a kind of energy in our lives, we can see that everything depends upon how we use it. If we understand the conditions that support our happiness, we can use our money to establish and nurture those conditions.

The unifying theme of these lessons is that wealth-building is world-building. In the process of building wealth, you are in the process of building your life. If the process is not pleasurable, it is pointless. If the process is not pleasurable, you are doing it wrong. This month's lesson is brief but very important. It teaches how to make wealth-building FUN.

PERSONAL WEALTH AND PERSONAL GROWTH

The psychologist Abraham Maslow talked about needs that people have beyond immediate survival needs such as air, water, food and shelter. When those basic needs are met, our attention turns to the fulfillment of social needs for friendship and intimacy, intellectual and aesthetic stimulation and personal growth. The ability to fulfill all of these needs is wealth. Money is a means of creating that wealth. To repeat something that was said in Lesson Two:

[H]aving more money really means having more freedom and power to do the things that you want to do. We need money to survive but it also helps us to thrive and to fully enjoy the pleasures of life. Money is a means to purchase material luxuries, of course, but it also facilitates having fun with our family and friends, learning new things, supporting causes that we care about and improving our worlds in every way.

Managing your money more wisely and accumulating more of it is simply a means of gaining more control and more freedom in your life. It gives you more time and more options in exploring and satisfying your personal needs and likewise so in creating the life that enables you to become the truest and fullest expression of yourself.

That is what Deep Indulgence is all about and why it is explicitly included in the spending plan described in last month's lesson. To be truly wealthy, it is not enough to simply accumulate enough money to live comfortably and pleasurably. You must seek out, both within and beyond yourself, the life that most fully and deeply satisfies your unique and personal needs.

WHERE TO BUY HAPPINESS

One way to use money to increase happiness that was already mentioned in last month's lesson is by contributing to charity. In the context of this lesson, we want to stress that you consider charitable giving carefully and give to causes that you truly care about. Giving to causes that you do not truly, personally and deeply care about - regardless of how worthy you may intellectually consider them to be - will on some level feel like an obligation. Giving to a cause that you truly resonate with will make you feel good on all levels.

Perhaps the most effective way to buy happiness is to lessen your focus on things and spend more on the dynamics of living. Having the things that you need to live in comfort and quality is good. Neither is there anything wrong with owning some designer clothing, high-end toys and shiny baubles (go back to Lesson Two if you think that there is). However, even if something like collecting jewelry, special cars, fine art or antique furniture is truly your real passion in life, you will still increase your happiness by using most of your extra spending on creating memories and accomplishments. Beyond the point of securing survival and comfort, good times are truer wealth than stuff.

Things like travel, continuing education, taking up an art or sport and enjoying special times with friends and family - perhaps in combination with travel, learning and art or sport - are the most commonly described sources of happy experiences that can be facilitated by having money. You will want to explore such things for yourself and tune into your own personal wavelength of happiness. These are your Deep Indulgences.

The mistake that is often made in trying to buy happiness is that money is randomly spent (as it can be, according to the means of the spender) on the immediate gratification of petty whims. In contrast, the process taught in these lessons works to establish the conditions for happiness by focusing on real needs and deep desires - things that are unique and personal to you - combined with a sense of accomplishment by working over time for their best fulfillment.

MAKING IT INTO PLAY

If you go back to the questions that were asked in the first two lessons and think about the bad habits and attitudes that people can have with regard to money, it makes sense that many people to some degree expect the work involved in building wealth to be uncomfortable, difficult or simply boring. By now, you should have made some progress in transforming any bad attitudes or habits of your own and have a new viewpoint on the process. You can further build upon that new viewpoint by invoking a sense of play and turning your wealth-building into a game.

Just look at last month's lesson. Frugality and thrift are often thought of in terms of being cheap or miserly and can be associated with grim mindsets of fear and lack. For some, this may be true. However, when you are coming up with new ways to get more value for the money that you spend, how is that not a game? The game is to get more out of your money while spending less of it. Every bargain is a win and your savings can be applied to increasing your overall "score" - your net worth. Along the way, your Deep Indulgences can and should be thought of as bonuses.

Later in this course, in addition to the creativity that you are currently bringing to saving the money that you already have, you will be bringing even more creativity into making more money. If you have cultivated your sense of play with regard to wealth-building, the game will become even more exciting then.

TAKING ACTION

1. Think about all of the different kinds of needs that you might have as listed above: survival needs (such as food, clothing and shelter), social needs for friendship and intimacy, intellectual and aesthetic stimulation and personal growth. Include FUN. Daydream and fantasize about the specific ways of fulfilling those needs that would be most uniquely satisfying and stimulating for you. Describe these in your journal.

2. Think again about charitable giving and what causes resonate with you most strongly. Adjust your giving accordingly.

3. Having given them time to percolate in your mind, go back to Step 1 and think about how you might make those dreams and fantasies actually happen. Compose a list of possible Deep Indulgences. Choose one or two to start saving for now.

4. Use your enthusiasm for your Deep Indulgence to motivate your savings. Do not look at money put aside now simply as money put aside, know that it is a dream coming true in the future.

5. Going forward, as you accumulate Deep Indulgence experiences, make notes of your experiences and reflections in your journal. Maybe you will not enjoy some as much as you thought that you would. Maybe you will really enjoy some of them even more than you expected to. Look especially for patterns that can help you to seek out even deeper indulgences of your truest Self.

6. Both now and with the lessons still to come, think about all of the ways that wealth-building can be seen as a game. Take this perspective and apply it as you take all of the actions suggested at the end of each lesson.

NOTES

NOTES

NOTES

NOTES

LESSON FIVE: INTRODUCTION TO MARKETS AND CAPITAL

As relative beginners moving forward in our process of understanding how wealth is created and accumulated, terms like "market" and "capital" may seem remote and abstract in comparison with our own experience. Culturally, these terms may seem to be connected to the activities of business moguls and tycoons and not to the economic activity of the average person. Nothing could be further from the truth.

In last month's lesson, you were advised and encouraged to enhance your wealth-creation experience by looking at it as a game. Markets are the playing fields or game environments in which wealth-creation takes place. EVERYONE plays a role within markets. Capital is like the power level or other resources in a game that allow you to play. It facilitates and fuels the productivity of markets.

MARKETS DEFINED

In origin, the word "market" is related to words like "merchant" and "merchandise" which all refer to trade. A market is simply a place, social network, institution or other system in which people come together to trade. The General Market, what is meant by economists when simply referring to "The Market," is merely the sum of all economic activity. This General Market includes all smaller markets within it, such as stock, commodity and currency markets, industry or product-specific markets, physical market places (such as agoras and flea markets, fairs, farmer's markets, shopping centers or malls), internet commerce, barter exchanges and even underground "black markets."

PRICE AND SPONTANEOUS ORDER

They key to understanding markets is in the balance of supply and demand. People have goods or services that other people want, so there is trade or commerce. Understandably, if a good or service is very much wanted but rare, its price will be higher. If a good or service is not generally wanted or is in abundant supply, its price will be lower.

The price reflects how much the good or service is valued. Buyers and sellers negotiate this value until they find a price that they both agree upon and then make the exchange. As many exchanges occur within a market, the price of any good or service comes to conform to a general average. This average is a dynamic point of equilibrium that rises and falls with shifts in supply and demand.

This kind of emergent, dynamic equilibrium has a name: Spontaneous Order.

Spontaneous Order is the self-organized emergence of order out of seeming disorder. It is the novel state or pattern that emerges from the free interaction of elements within a system. As a process, this free interaction allows for evolution through variation, competition, feedback and adaptation. It is thus dynamic and tends to create abundance as many new and unexpected innovations and values emerge from its rich complexity. Other fundamental examples of Spontaneous Order include the evolution of life and ecosystems and the development of language.

Perhaps the earliest to write about Spontaneous Order were the Daoist philosophers of ancient China, notably Laozi and Zhuangzhi (also commonly known as Lao-tse and Chuang-tse). Laozi wrote that to grasp the world is to lose it and that the world is won by letting things alone. More clearly, Zhuangzhi, in particular, emphasized that good order results spontaneously when things are let alone.

As goods and services are matched up with needs and desires, exchanges of value are made, with the sum of all commercial activity making up what we call the General Market. In a free market, the flows and systems for facilitating trade and commerce evolve through the same mechanisms of Spontaneous Order previously mentioned: variation, competition, feedback and adaptation. Adam Smith, the author of *The Wealth of Nations*, perceived this process and famously called it the "Invisible Hand."

The price mechanism described above is one example of how this "Invisible Hand" works within markets. You may remember that the importance of this price mechanism was stressed back in Lesson One in connection with the evolution of money (another example of Spontaneous Order), where it was said:

When exchanges are made in money, the exchange ratios of all goods and services can be compared in the language of prices. This allows farmers, craftsmen, merchants and all other businessmen to calculate their expenses and profits, which facilitates the formation of an elaborate structure of production.

TWO FALLACIES

There are two common misunderstandings that affect the way that some people perceive markets and how they function.

The first misunderstanding is in viewing trade as what is known as a "zero-sum game." A zero-sum game is where the total gains and losses balance to zero · every gain is the result of a corresponding loss. People that hold this view believe that no one can benefit except at the expense of someone else, so they see every exchange as having a winner and a loser. Barring fraud or coercion, though, both sides of an exchange are winners because they both receive what they want or need. This will be explained more fully below.

This misunderstanding is related to another one: the idea of objective or intrinsic value. This is the idea that goods have a "true" value that is objective or intrinsic within the good, itself, and that prices should reflect this supposed value. Perhaps the best-known theory of this type is the labor theory of value, which holds that things are valuable because of the labor that goes into their production.

However, the truth is that value is always subjective because it reflects the particular wants and needs of a particular valuer at a specific time. Value exists solely in the mind of a unique person in relation to the circumstances of their own life or business.

When these misunderstandings are the basis of interfering with the spontaneous order of the market · such as a goverment or other entity establishing a fixed, artificial price on something (say, labor, as a common example) · the interference can result in creating the problem that it was meant to avoid. The win-win game of trade and commerce can become, in fact, a win-lose or even lose-lose scenario. This stands to reason because the artificial, externally imposed price may no longer reflect the actual value of the good or service to either one or both of the parties involved in the exchange. The market, which exists to satisfy the wants and needs of its participants, no longer reflects the values of those participants.

Gennadi Gerasimov, foreign affairs spokesman for then-Soviet leader Mikhail Gorbachev, once opened a talk at an international conference with a joke about a future in which the Soviet Union had successfully conquered every country in the world except for New Zealand, which it had chosen not to invade. The reason? So that they would know the market price of goods.

It is important to understand that while price and value are intimately related, they are not synonymous or identical. In every exchange, because value is subjective, each participant is getting MORE value than they are offering. If this were not so, there would be no incentive or reason for the exchange. If a buyer purchases a calf for $200, the buyer obviously values the calf more than the money. Likewise, the money is worth more to the seller than the calf is. Otherwise, each would keep what they already have. The same would be true in a barter exchange of, say, two pigs for the calf. Each participant walks away from the exchange WEALTHIER than they were before. Again, EACH participant walks away from the exchange WEALTHIER than they were before, and this is so in EVERY act of free exchange that occurs in life.

CAPITAL AND PROFIT

Of course, another key element to understand is Capital.

Capital refers to resources other than labor used in production of goods or services. This includes things like tools or machinery but also the money used to purchase such things and to otherwise get the enterprise running. Even when capital is not money, as such, it is still considered in monetary terms for calculation purposes in running a business. Capital is the sum of financial resources risked in an enterprise by entrepreneurs and other investors (who are also in this sense entrepreneurs) in the hope of a returning profit. Profit can also be used as new capital. As the economist Ludwig von Mises succinctly described it:

"Capital goods come into existence by saving. A part of the goods produced is withheld from immediate consumption and employed for processes the fruits of which will only mature at a later date. All material civilization is based upon this

'capitalistic' approach to the problems of production."

An interesting word to consider here is "Extropy" - the opposite of "entropy" (disorder or decay). Extropy has been defined by the philosopher Max More for his own purposes as "the extent of a living or organizational system's intelligence, functional order, vitality, energy, life, experience, and capacity and drive for improvement and growth." It is also worth noting that More identified Spontaneous Order as a key principle in relation to Extropy.

We might think of capital (and profit used as new capital) as the increasing Extropy within the system of economic activity (the General Market). In this sense, when we talk about wealth-building, we do not mean just the personal accumulation of money and goods. We also refer to something that is being actually created.

As a result, we live today awash in an ocean of wealth and capital that has been gradually accumulating since primitive man first learned to create tools and to cultivate crops.

SAVINGS AND INVESTMENT

You now perhaps understand capital in a new way and can see how it applies to your own life and wealth.

There are only so many hours in a day that you can work. By saving and investing some of your money, that money can be working for you and earning more money for you. You will remember from Lesson Three that the essential formula for building wealth is to produce more than you consume. When looking at the two sides of that formula, we initially focused on reducing consumption because increasing what you keep matters more than simply increasing what you bring in without regard to its retention. However, investing allows you to use some of your savings to increase your income. This is your own capital and can work for you as described above.

First, though, focus on your security. You want to have a minimum six-month emergency fund and to have payed off your debts before you begin to get seriously involved with investing. You might also give serious thought to making home ownership a priority. Owning your home means an end to rent and will increase your net worth (your score in the game of building wealth). Your home can also serve as an asset in operating your own business, either by using it as the place of business or by using the home as collateral for a loan (though new debt should be a last resort, of course). You might even rent your first home as an additional source of income if you later move into a new one.

Perhaps the most common way to profit from your

savings is through the use of certificates of deposit. A certificate of deposit is essentially a loan made to a bank or credit union, where you deposit a specified amount of money in the bank for a specified period of time. By agreeing to leave the money for that time period, you receive a higher rate of interest on the money than you would in a savings account. Certificates of deposit are insured and carry virtually no risk.

There are two types of account that are used by many people to facilitate saving for retirement: the 401(k) and the Individual Retirement Arrangement or Account (IRA).

The 401(k) account is named for the section of the tax code that allows for it. The money placed into the 401(k) account is not taxed until it is withdrawn, and neither is the interest earned. These plans are usually administered by the employer, who may match employee contributions to it, with the money usually invested in mutual funds (see below). If the 401(k) option is available in your workplace, maximize it by contributing up to your employer's match. If you are Self-employed, you can also set up one of these accounts and make contributions as both employee and employer.

The IRA is a holding account where you can place a variety of assets and investments, including real estate. In a traditional IRA, the money that you invest is not taxed until it is withdrawn at retirement. With another type, the Roth IRA, the investments are not tax-deductible but can be withdrawn tax-free at retirement.

These savings accounts make use of the power of compounding, which is the marriage of money and time through re-investing. As interest is earned, the total amount of money increases, which results in more interest being earned.

One very dramatic way to understand how compounding works is to imagine having a penny that doubles every day. How long would it take you to become a millionaire? Well, the first week would look like this: .01, .02, .04, .08, .16, .32 and .64. Only 64 cents. The second week would see $1.28, 2.56, 5.12, 10.24, 20.48, 40.96 and 81.92. Much better, but still not what most of us would consider to be great wealth. Over the third week, you would see $163.84, 327.68, 655.36, 1310.72, 2621.44, 5242.88 and 10,485.76. Something is definitely happening now! By the end of the fourth week, you would have $1,342,177.28!

Now, obviously, you are not going to double your money every day or even every year through these accounts. However, you will experience the same kind of accelerating upward curve (albeit more modestly) by taking advantage of the power of compounding. To do so, it is important that you begin IMMEDIATELY. Consider the doubling pennies that made you a millionaire in twenty-eight days. If you had delayed starting by just ONE DAY, you would have had only $671,088.64 at the end of the fourth week. Similarly, every year that you wait to begin using compound interest can result in having considerably less money when you wish to retire. Starting EARLY is much more important than starting big. Balance starting this kind of saving as soon as possible with the other important, initial priorities such as your emergency fund, paying off debt and purchasing a home.

Common types of investments include bonds, stocks and mutual funds. A bond is essentially a loan. In purchasing the bond, you are lending that money to a business or government to be repaid with interest. Bonds are much like certificates of deposit but carry slightly more risk. Stocks are shares in the ownership of businesses. Owning stock in a company allows you to receive profits called dividends that the company pays out to shareholders (stock owners). Stocks are riskier than bonds. Mutual funds are collections of stocks and bonds, selected by a professional manager and made up from the pooled money of a number of investors. There are many types of mutual funds focusing on specific types of investments, specific industries and even serving particular economic theories and religious beliefs. The combination of bonds, stocks, mutual funds and other assets that one might own make up what is known as a *portfolio*, after a type of briefcase.

One type of alternative investing is by collecting art, antiques or other rare items. This type of investing can be very risky, but can provide an opportunity to capitalize on your unique passions and personal knowledge. The same can be said of starting your own business, a topic that is so important that it will be covered in some detail in future lessons.

TAKING ACTION

1. Consider the two fallacies described above - that trade is a zero-sum game and that value is objective - and watch for them in your own thinking. If they are present, handle them in the same way that handling anti-money attitudes was described in Lesson Two.

2. Go back to Lesson Three and look at the material there from the perspective of further increasing your savings and capital. Include the extra-financial resources described at the end of the lesson and start thinking about how you can use them to increase your savings and/or income. In other words, keep doing what that lesson suggests, but do it now with an eye toward building capital and more active future expansion.

3. Look into using a 401(k) and IRA, take advantage of compounding your savings as soon as possible and then research other types of investments that you might want to include in your portfolio. You have a basic understanding of these things now, if you did not before, and can research them more fully.

4. Continue to enhance your wealth-building experience by approaching it as a game, as described in last month's lesson.

NOTES

NOTES

NOTES

NOTES

LESSON SIX: YOUR DEEPER RELATIONSHIP WITH MARKETS

In this lesson, many of the ideas and activities presented in the earlier lessons culminate in a "Big Picture" while also setting up the further work of the final three lessons to come.

You may have noticed that the titles of this lesson and the previous one reflect the titles of the first two lessons in this course. Before starting this lesson, it would be to your benefit to return to Lesson Two and review the "Pith of Civilization" section so as to re-familiarize yourself with the ideas presented there.

A CONTINUUM OF INDIVIDUAL, SOCIAL AND MATERIAL DIMENSIONS

Lesson Two referred to money having personal, exchange and commodity aspects. It was said then:

Keeping these factors in mind, then, we can see that in money there is a meeting of purpose, energy and substance. In effect, money acts as a force of creation and transformation. So, when we talk about wealth-building, what we really mean in the ultimate sense is WORLD-building, with money as the means for building worlds and worlds-within-worlds.

This is why the economist Ludwig von Mises said that Economics "is the philosophy of human life and action and concerns everybody and everything. It is the pith of civilization and of Man's human existence."

We find even more truth in Mises' statement when we see that markets - and especially the overall General Market - have these same aspects. There is an Individual dimension made up of the particular needs, desires, efforts and abilities of unique Individuals, a Social dimension in which these things are matched up for exchange and a Material dimension made up of physical resources and goods. These three dimensions define the full continuum of existence. Consider: virtually every waking moment involves some form of production, exchange or consumption of value, far beyond what we usually think of in terms of buying and selling. When we use terms like "Market" or "Society" (or even "Life"), the line between these things is extremely blurry and they would perhaps more properly be considered to be different ways of describing the same thing.

So, to say that wealth-building is world-building is not just a poetic metaphor but is quite literal. To be as effective as possible in building wealth, it is important to understand the market continuum in this way and to master its three dimensions.

ECONOMY VS. CATALLAXY

The terms "economy" and "economics" derive from the Greek word *oikonomia*, which referred to the management or direction of a single household. The economist Friedrich Hayek, who wrote about Spontaneous Order in economics and society, felt that these terms are actually misleading when it comes to describing the larger, more complex phenomena of markets involving many participants with diverse needs and goals. Instead, Hayek proposed the use of alternative terms like "catallaxy" and "catallactics" that he derived from the Greek word *katallasso*, meaning "to exchange." Catallaxy, in Hayek's view, is the spontaneous order brought about by the mutual adjustment of many individual economies in a market.

The original word *katallasso* also has some very important secondary meanings of "to make friends" and "to admit into the community." In connection with these meanings, it is worthwhile to consider the old saying that when goods do not cross borders, soldiers will. We might also expect the opposite to be true, that when goods DO cross borders, soldiers will NOT · or will at least be less likely to. Trade being so essential to survival and thriving in life, people are not happy for it to be disrupted. This is not only true on the level of nations or, again, only in the usual terms of buying and selling. The exchanges of value between Individuals are what form the relationships between them and these bonds are the building blocks of social order. In the fullest sense, all human interactions can be seen as a form of commerce.

"Catallaxy" may not replace "economy" in our language anytime soon, but it is very helpful to be familiar with this term. Integrating the catallactic view of markets into your thinking will give you an advantage in mastering the Social dimension of the market continuum as described above.

LIFE IS COMMERCE

If all of this is understood, we can see that the idea of exchange or trade is an important ethical principle as well as a practical one for maximizing our happiness in life, which is the ultimate value underlying all forms of wealth. This does not mean keeping an obsessive mental ledger to record all of our interactions and be sure that each one is perfectly balanced down to the minutest degree. However, we do want to be sure that we are not taken advantage of and we want to be sure that we have value in the lives of our associates.

As an extreme example, we all know about the friend, relative or significant other that is simply a black hole of Need. They always need something, be it money or some kind of help or just "emotional support" - but never seem to be around when we need something in return. It does us no good to have these people around and we certainly do not want to BE that person. Inequality of exchange in relationships is not always so obvious, though. In some cases, we may not be giving enough or may be giving too much just out of inattention to what is happening. However, even if an unequal relationship is not recognized consciously by either party, there will still be a subliminal dis-ease in the relationship.

Consciously clearing and balancing relationships as exchanges of value ensures that the relationship continues to have worth for both parties. This is a simple way to increase and maintain social wealth, while integrating it as a personality trait will also assist you in making more money. This constitution of yourself as a creator and trader of value and applying that to increasing your income will be the focus for the remainder of this course.

TAKING ACTION

1. As in Lesson Two, be mindful of opportunities to actively appreciate money and wealth as they arise. Extend that exercise to an appreciation for living in an extremely complex economy (or catallaxy). Contemplate the many opportunities that people have, both in their choices for work and in the culture that they can enjoy. Watch for occasions to notice these things and make a mental note of praise and thankfulness when they appear.

2. Review the explanation of Spontaneous Order in Lesson Five. Contemplate the distinction between "Economy" and "Catallaxy" in the context of Spontaneous Order. When people speak of "The Economy," stop and think in terms of Catallaxy.

How does that affect your viewpoint? Does it make you feel more empowered, personally, as a participant? What other insights does it trigger?

3. Examine your perception of and reactions to the ideas in this lesson. Similarly to the anti-money thoughts described in Lesson Two, do you find that you hold anti-commerce attitudes or beliefs that inhibit your willingness to fully participate in the market of exchange? If so, how might you clear such attitudes and beliefs? If necessary, begin to do so.

4. Think about both your work and your personal relationships as exchanges of value. What do you provide in these exchanges? Be aware of your own worth and value and consider how you might want to increase and change it. How can you offer more now? How can you increase what you have to offer in the future? Take action on what you discover and decide.

5. Once again, think about your relationships and how they may have already changed and may continue to change as your wealth increases. You will see now that this is a bigger issue than handling just the people with anti-money and anti-wealth attitudes that were mentioned in Lesson Two. Now, the focus is more broadly on exchange. Look closely at all of your relationships, both personal and professional. What are you getting and what are you giving? Are the exchanges balanced? Should you be giving more, as suggested above? If you are not getting enough, would it be

more appropriate to try to get more, give less or simply withdraw from the relationship? Consider these questions and adjust your relationships accordingly.

NOTES

NOTES

NOTES

NOTES

LESSON SEVEN: PROFILE OF A WEALTH-BUILDER

At this point, you have made some changes to your financial behavior but you have also begun to make some changes in yourself. You have a basic understanding of what money and markets are and you have taken action to create a good psychological relationship with them. You have worked to become disciplined in tracking your money, in saving and in cultivating frugality and thrift. This is a strong foundation.

Now, we can also add four key traits to your personal transformation that will greatly empower you as a wealth-builder: Self-determinism, long-term thinking, cultivating multiple streams of income and protecting your assets.

SELF-DETERMINISM AND LONG-TERM THINKING

The first trait of a wealth-builder that we will describe is Self-determinism, and this may be the most important trait. Self-determinism means actively creating your own identity, coming to your own conclusions and choosing your own actions rather than passively allowing other people or your environment to determine who you are, what is right or possible for you or what you should do. Self-determinism means taking responsibility for creating your own existence.

That does not mean ignoring reality, of course, but it does mean making your own luck. Whether outside conditions are good or bad, there are always intelligent choices to be made and benefits to be gained. It has been said that luck is what happens when preparation meets opportunity, so the wealth-builder cultivates knowledge and takes Self-determined action.

Another important wealth-building trait is long-term thinking. A key aspect of long-term thinking is having goals. Short-term thinking is generally motivated by the drive to satisfy random wants in the present. Even long-term thinkers are motivated in this way and occasionally act accordingly. That is alright but it becomes a problem as a way of life in which people wander aimlessly and scatter their energies. Long-term thinkers have a VISION of the life that they want and the things that they want to accomplish. Your goals provide a stable focus for your values and efforts so that your investments of time and energy result in productive ends.

Moreover, another aspect of long-term thinking that is more specific to wealth-building is to focus on activities that will return income for many years from a single effort or investment rather than activities that provide a one-time pay-off. One example would be buying a house to rent to others, as opposed to buying a house in order to "flip" it for a higher re-sell price.

MULTIPLE STREAMS OF INCOME

Relying upon a single source of income such as a job or even a single business means DEPENDENCE and the Self-determined wealth-builder will not tolerate that. Also, either intuitively or explicitly, they know that wealth-building is world-building and their ability to see and create opportunities from the stuff of life around them is holistic and always active. Serious wealth-builders create multiple streams of income. Moreover, as long-term thinkers, they seek to create multiple streams of PASSIVE income.

Active income streams involve doing either the same kind of work for multiple businesses (your own and/or someone else's) or doing different kinds of work (again, either for yourself or for someone else). Passive income streams, once established, continue to provide income with little or no further effort on your part.

Examples of multiple streams of active income include sports figures that also endorse products, authors that also do paid speaking engagements or anyone that has a second job or side business. Examples of passive income sources include investments, rental properties and book royalties. Even your emergency fund and other savings can be a small source of passive income if the money is collecting interest.

ASSET PROTECTION

Serious wealth-builders also take steps to protect their wealth. Broadly defined, asset protection includes:

A. Understanding taxes and the use of legal and appropriate tax planning strategies, structures or techniques to minimize the depletion of assets - which further includes developing a proper estate plan to transfer assets to your children or other heirs with minimal costs.

B. Having the best insurance that you can for your health, life, vehicle(s), home(s) and other personal property, as well as for your business assets and/or whatever liability or professional insurance is appropriate for your work.

C. Putting your income and property out of the reach of creditors and lawsuits.

Taxes, death or illness, accidents, natural disasters and legal dramas can all have a devastating impact upon the wealth that you have created for yourself and your family. They should be given consideration in your long-term thinking and planning.

TAKING ACTION

1. Make a list of everyone that you have considered to be an authority or expert on the subjects of money and wealth. This list would include your parents and other relatives, peers, teachers, book authors, journalists and so on. Take a few moments to reflect on each person in turn. What do you think their vision and intentions were with regard to their advice? What are your vision and intentions on the subject? How are they different? With every Individual being different and having a life made up of different elements and conditions, can any two Individuals share the EXACT same vision and intentions? With regard to each person, can you think of an instance (or more than one) where you KNOW that you knew better, at least for yourself? The aim of this exercise is not necessarily to invalidate these people, their visions, intentions or knowledge. The aim is to put "authorities" into perspective as resources that you can evaluate from your own Self-determined position.

2. Based upon your Deep Indulgence experiences

and everything else that you have learned, start creating a vision of what you want your life to look like twenty years from now. In alignment with that vision, what do you want your life to look like ten years from now? What about five years from now? What part of your vision can you create this year? Use the process for creating goals given in Appendix One to create goals for the next one, five, ten and twenty-year periods. From this list of goals, create plans for action and begin doing what is necessary. Do not be afraid to revise your vision and goals as you both learn more about yourself and gain greater knowledge of the means to your ends, but continue to be decisive. Use new understanding to increase your focus. Think things through and also plan for worst-case scenarios.

3. Consider various sources of new income that you might establish. Which ones appeal to you? Where and how might they fit into your long-term vision? How might they support or enhance that vision? Do more research and incorporate your answers into your long-term plans. In particular, continue to think about both your work and your personal relationships as exchanges of value as you did in Lesson Six. How can you offer more now? How can you increase what you have to offer in the future? Be aware of your own worth and value and consider how you might want to increase and change it. This activity will continue and assume new importance

in next month's lesson.

4. Specific strategies for handling taxes, estate planning and other forms of asset protection are too advanced and complex for discussing here in this lesson. They depend on where you live as well as the specific details of your own situation and are also constantly changing. However, you can take action in this area now by seeking out more information and assistance. This means consulting with qualified professionals: an accountant, an attorney, appropriate insurance agents and perhaps even an asset protection specialist. Find these professionals by seeking out and weighing a number of recommendations from people with situations that are similar to yours. Do further research to help you in making the best choices in assembling this team. Also, make sure that your emergency fund is in good shape.

NOTES

NOTES

NOTES

NOTES

LESSON EIGHT: CREATING VALUE AND INCREASING INCOME

This is the lesson that you have probably been looking for from the beginning. You should now understand, though, that there is a context to building and maintaining wealth and that it is not just a simple matter of getting more money. Your work with the previous lessons will have transformed your existence into a more fit receptacle for wealth and transformed you into a more effective wealth-builder.

However, with that being accomplished - or at least firmly and decidedly coming into being - you can now more productively make use of extra income and add it to net worth in measuring your wealth and its growth. Avoiding the opposing extremes of either having a high income with a lot of wasteful spending or debt OR having lots of assets and no money, you can place yourself in the flow of balanced wealth.

You can do this by increasing your pay at a job or by seeking the freedom of the entrepreneur.

Personal fulfillment can be found on either path if your work aligns with your interests, talents and authentic purpose in life.

THE ULTIMATE RESOURCE

Wealth is that which enhances our existence. With the few, basic exceptions of oxygen, water and other simple survival fare such as fruits, nuts or grubs, natural resources alone are not wealth. Wealth has to be created, which requires effort or labor. However, labor alone is not enough to create wealth, either. A horse can pull a cart, but the horse can not drive the cart and it certainly can not invent a cart. The ultimate resource, the one that makes all wealth possible, is the Self-determined mind and its powers of reason and creativity.

To hunt or grow food, to build shelter and to weave cloth all required these powers, both to understand how to do these things and to create the tools for accomplishing them. Without the powers of the mind, the metals that go into everything from a knife to a car, to a skyscraper and to a spaceship would just be rocks.

The ultimate resource is the mind that directs labor to productive ends. The ultimate resource is the ability to look at the stuff and experiences that make up the world around us and to see how they can be shaped, assembled, recombined and redirected to produce more valuable stuff and more valuable experiences.

CREATING VALUE

Value is simply a scale of how useful or important something is to someone. Value is created by creating something that you or someone else needs or wants. Another way to create value is to improve upon something valuable that already exists, raising quality and increasing its value. Value can also be increased by just improving delivery somehow or by finding a way to offer the same quality at a lower price.

One of the most harmful ideas that people have about wealth - and one of the most common - is that there is a shared, finite store of it from which we all must draw, like dividing up a pie. The immediate problem with this "pie" concept is that it puts people into the mindset of the "zero-sum game" fallacy that was described in Lesson Five, where every gain implies a corresponding loss. On the personal level, it imparts a dire tone to our attempts to build wealth by evoking a struggle for the same resources that everyone else is trying to obtain. This may contribute to the formation of psychological barriers that can prevent an Individual from even trying to build more wealth. Moreover, the implied conflict encourages unethical behaviors at all levels of society, generally, while also making it possible for a "politics of envy" to be exploited by those who might seek to further profit unethically from the corresponding rifts in society (catallaxy). To reiterate what was said in Lesson Five:

A zero-sum game is where the total gains and losses balance to zero - every gain is the result of a corresponding loss. People that hold this view believe that no one can benefit except at the expense of someone else, so they see every exchange as having a winner and a loser. Barring fraud or coercion, though, both sides of an exchange are winners because they both receive what they want or need.

(You may wish to review the "Two Fallacies" section of Lesson Five.)

Without engaging in a lot of social or political arguments, we can see from the perspective on wealth that we have been crafting over the course of these lessons that the proper ethical distinction should be between those who make and trade wealth and those who take it by fraud or theft. Both types, Makers and Takers, can be found at all levels of society (catallaxy). When economic (catallactic) affairs run justly, Makers are in a position to have more money precisely because of the value that they have created for others. Moreover, by combining the Ultimate Resource described above with the subjective nature of value in exchange, the entire "pie" - the total, overall pool of wealth in society - continually GROWS because of their efforts. On a personal level, the greater your ability to create value is, the greater your ability to increase your own wealth will be in whatever economic (catallactic) conditions you may find yourself.

You have the ability to create value. You can look for the good in each situation and try to expand it or creatively put some new good into the situation. This can be done to turn around what appear to be bad situations but it can also be done to make good situations better. It is sometimes said that customers really only ever buy two things: solutions to problems and pleasurable experiences. If you can provide either of these things, you can create value for yourself and others. Because of the differences in people, and because value is subjective, the variety of possible problems to be solved and pleasurable experiences to be had is obviously vast. This means that the variety of opportunities is vast.

Creating value in your work is the way to create wealth, both for yourself and the wider world. That is, creating value in the form of products and services that you can exchange for money will increase your personal wealth but you should also understand that the value created is not limited to that specific commercial exchange. It adds to the overall wealth of the world, however incrementally. So, to create value and wealth, invent something new in your own field, add some new innovation to the mix, find standards that you can raise or even create a new field altogether.

ENTREPRENEURSHIP AND SELF-ACTUALIZATION

In Lesson Two, we talked about why building wealth is really important:

For you, personally, having more money really means having more freedom and power to do the things that you want to do. We need money to survive but it also helps us to thrive and to fully enjoy the pleasures of life. Money is a means to purchase material luxuries, of course, but it also facilitates having fun with our family and friends, learning new things, supporting causes that we care about and improving our worlds in every way.

So, the question of how much money you need depends entirely on how much it will cost for you to be the most YOU that you can be and to live that life fully and completely. In any case, this means that you need to be financially independent enough to live the life that truly and fully reflects you and is truly and fully yours.

Unless you are the CEO of a major, multinational

corporation, you are not going to become financially independent solely through working at a job for someone else. Unless you already have a lot of money to start with, you are also *probably* not going become financially independent by investing alone. If you want to become financially independent, you need to be in business for yourself.

An Individual who organizes and manages a business undertaking, assuming the risk for the sake of the profit, is known as an *entrepreneur.* This French term is related to the word "enterprise" and so contains ideas of action and creativity. This creativity and action is applied to satisfying (or improving the satisfaction of) some social need or market demand in the form of a product or service.

So, immediately, the entrepreneur is creating new value for customers. However, if the enterprise is larger than the entrepreneur can handle alone, value is also created in the form of jobs and wages for employees. Moreover, some forms of value creation can change the world · just consider the social impact of such products as the telephone, airplane, penicillin or the personal computer.

Good examples of how to progress entrepreneurial activity in this way are Peter Thiel and Elon Musk, two of the co·counders of PayPal. PayPal is a relatively simple service that allows people to make payments or otherwise transfer money through the internet. It fulfilled a basic need and helped to facilitate the explosive growth of internet commerce. As this is written, Peter Thiel has since become an investor in a variety of social media networks (including Facebook) and is an active philanthropist, providing money for efforts in anti-aging research and seasteading. Elon Musk has co-founded Tesla Motors, which produces electric cars, and is opening the way into worlds beyond Earth as the founder of SpaceX, creators of the Dragon spacecraft. Thiel and Musk are both on the board of directors of Halcyon Molecular, a biotechnology company that aims to help genetic research by improving DNA sequencing. This is New Wealth building New Worlds, indeed.

Maybe your success will not be on such a grand scale. Then again, maybe it will be. That depends entirely upon what you want to do. In any case, it IS entirely possible for you to make an impact within the scale of your own vision. The extreme division of labor within our society acts as a great force for unleashing human potential by giving people the option to do work that they are particularly suited for. If you can focus this force into an entrepreneurial vision by matching something that you are passionate about - maybe even your unique Life Purpose - with a social need or desire (market demand), and act upon it, you can actually get paid to live out your dreams.

Or, maybe you just start where you can, in the general area, and work your way toward that goal.

This is a path of personal growth and fulfillment. By increasing your Self-knowledge, you can come to a conscious understanding of your core values. Using the money that you set aside for Deep Indulgence (Lesson Three), you can explore and pursue a variety of enjoyable activities that reflect or support those core values. From these activities, you can select the ones that best match your strongest interests and talents. These are the activities where your Life Purpose may be found and you can find a job or create a business in doing them.

The thing, itself, does not necessarily even have to be something completely unique. However, if you can do it better than your competition or in a new and unique way, you will still emerge as something special and have a good chance at great success.

TAKING ACTION

1. In Lesson Two, you made the effort to be mindful of opportunities to actively appreciate money and wealth as they arose. In Lesson Six, you extended that exercise to an appreciation for living in an extremely complex economy (catallaxy). Repeat this

practice again this month. However, this time, be sure to also observe that all created goods have their origin in the mind. This is especially true in cities, where almost everything that you see began in someone's imagination. Think about that.

2. Begin to quest for your Life Purpose. How long this will take depends upon your level of honest Self-knowledge. First, ask yourself what your talents are. What do you think that you are good at? What things have others complimented you on? You should also directly ask others what they think that you are good at. Write these things down in your journal, as many as you and the others can think of.

Next, create a similar list for the things that most interest you in life. What subject matter most interests you in books, films or other media? What do you like to talk about? What do you do for fun? What kinds of hobbies interest you? What have you been doing with your Deep Indulgence money and what have you learned from those experiences? Again, write down as many answers to these questions as you can think of.

The third step is to think about what activities you engage in (or could) that reflect your key passions and express your best talents or skills. How might these activities be turned into a job or business? Remember what was said above about customers only buying solutions to problems or pleasurable experiences. How can those be tied into these activities? When you find the best answer, you will know what you should do.

Start now. Maybe you will have to ease into it as a second job or small side business while maintaining your current job but START NOW.

3. If you want to increase job income, you will need to determine how you can make more money at your current job, whether you want to switch jobs or whether you want to take a second job while keeping your first one. Research how to re-negotiate your salary or negotiate a new one at a new job. Think about how you can increase your value to your employer. You want to realistically offer several times the monetary value of the increase that you are asking for, so be ready to show your employer how you can do that. Increasing your value as an employee may require further education, so find out if your employer offers tuition reimbursement.

4. Marshal your forces. Think about your knowledge and skills as you did above and back in Lesson Six. Apply them to the extra-financial resources that you listed back in Lesson Three or make a new list if necessary. Use these resources strategically in obtaining or creating the job or business of your dreams.

5. If you are starting a business or even just going for further training or education, you are going to need an increase in your capital. However, insofar as possible, you want obtain this capital without taking on debt. If your needs are relatively small, you might sell off your unneeded possessions or engage in part-time work on the side. You might also be able to fund your business or product through crowd funding. Crowd funding allows you to pool small contributions from many people in return for various rewards. There are currently quite a few web sites that facilitate this, including Kickstarter, ArtistShare, IndieGoGo and RocketHub. Of course, you can also seek out partners or other investors for larger-scale endeavors.

NOTES

NOTES

NOTES

NOTES

LESSON NINE: FORMING YOUR WEALTH-BUILDING ALLIANCE

In this course, you have twice been advised to consider your relationships with other people. In Lesson Two, you were advised to evaluate and adjust your social matrix with regard to attitudes about money and wealth in general. In Lesson Six, you were advised to do the same with regard to more specific attitudes about the nature of commerce. To the extent that you have taken action on that advice, you have probably already gained some experiential insight into how your social relationships can affect your wealth in both the financial and wider senses of the word.

In this final lesson, you will learn to further build upon this social foundation by establishing conscious and strategic alliances for creating, preserving and cultivating wealth.

LIFE, WEALTH, POWER AND RELATIONSHIPS

The continuous message running through this

entire course has been that wealth-building is world-building. Way back in Lesson Two, it was explained that:

For you, personally, having more money really means having more freedom and power to do the things that you want to do. We need money to survive but it also helps us to thrive and to fully enjoy the pleasures of life. Money is a means to purchase material luxuries, of course, but it also facilitates having fun with our family and friends, learning new things, supporting causes that we care about and improving our worlds in every way.

The famous German philosopher and psychologist, Friedrich Nietzsche, conceived the essence of life as what he called the "will to power." He said:

"My idea is that every specific body strives to be master over all space and to extend its force (its will to power) and to thrust back all that resists its extension. But it continually encounters similar efforts on the part of other bodies and ends by coming to an arrangement ('union') with those of them that are sufficiently related to it: Thus they conspire together for power."

Of course, as Individuals are very different, this will to power is expressed in very different ways and on different scales. Creating wealth is an expression of this same basic life-urge, as it is both the means and the substance of our survival and thriving in the material world. On this material foundation and within its spaces, energies and substance, we create the social, aesthetic and philosophical world(s) that we share with others.

The arrangements with others that Nietzsche speaks of are the basis of society and of the concept of Catallaxy that we have spoken of several times. It would be beneficial at this time to go back and review the "Economy vs. Catallaxy" section of Lesson Six.

Furthermore, though, when Nietzsche says that "sufficiently related" entities "conspire together for power," he introduces a new idea that we can use in our wealth-building efforts: the creation of intentional alliances among resonant Individuals for enhancing each other's wealth-building knowledge and activities. In Lesson Three, you were told:

You have certain resources available to you. You can gain the cooperation of others in the use of their resources. Not only can you use those resources in creating the life that you want, but you can use them to obtain or control MORE, NEW resources. You have the ability to utilize all of these resources to create practically anything that you want, and you have the ability to expand your creations virtually without limit and in all directions. Cultivate the habit of constantly looking for additional resources that you can utilize.

Now, in this lesson, the focus is on further maximizing this "bootstrapping" process by sharing it with others.

THE JUNTO AND THE MASTERMIND

The early American printer, inventor and political activist Benjamin Franklin has remained well-known for his worldly and practical wisdom. One of the key tools that Franklin used in becoming the man that he is remembered as today was a group that he founded in his youth. In 1727, at the age of 21, Franklin formed a club of other tradesmen for the purpose of mutual improvement. This group, known as the Junto or Leather Apron Club, met on Friday evenings to discuss issues of moral, political or natural philosophy as well as to exchange business knowledge and engage in mutual aid. Of the list of questions devised to guide the discussions, the following address the means by which wealth might be established:

Hath any citizen in your knowledge failed in his business lately, and what have you heard of the cause?

Have you lately heard of any citizen's thriving well, and by what means?

Have you lately heard how any present rich man, here or elsewhere, got his estate?

Do you know of any deserving young beginner lately set up, whom it lies in the power of the Junto any way to encourage?

Is there any man whose friendship you want, and which the Junto, or any of them, can procure for you?

In what manner can the Junto, or any of them, assist you in any of your honourable designs?

Have you any weighty affair in hand, in which you think the advice of the Junto may be of service?

The Junto lasted for four decades and was the root of the American Philosophical Society. Its history is interesting, but it was neither the first nor the last group of this type. Napoleon Hill, the author of the famous *Think and Grow Rich*, later put a spotlight on such groups and gave them a more precise focus by providing them with a name and a definition. Hill spoke of a type of group that he called a "Mastermind Alliance" and defined as "two or more minds working actively together in perfect harmony toward a common objective."

Today, there are several groups that model themselves on Franklin's Junto and many, many more that model themselves on Hill's Mastermind Alliance. In such an alliance, each Individual brings his or her own unique ideas, perspective, experience, knowledge and skills to the group. The result is a creative pool of resources that each member can draw benefit from. However, this pool of resources is *extropic* (Lesson Five) and can produce more than initially goes into it. As these diverse elements interact dynamically within the group, they play off of each other and new ideas and perspectives emerge.

GROUP TYPES, QUALITY OF MEMBERS AND KEEPING IT PROFESSIONAL

Mastermind groups can exist to achieve practically any type of goal. With regard to the work described in this course, you might find or create a Mastermind Alliance that focuses on any part of it. That includes starting and growing a business, investing, thrift and frugal living, handling psychological issues around money and wealth or any of the other topics that have been covered in these lessons. You might find or create a Mastermind Alliance that uses this course in its entirety as a guide, or introduce it to an existing group. You can participate in more than one Mastermind Alliance to cover whatever general or specific needs that you have. That is the first step, knowing what your needs are and what types of groups would benefit you now.

Next, you should have some understanding of the types of people that you want to work with. You will need to be able to get along with these people and work productively with them, but you do not want to work with people that are exactly like you. The diversity in groups is a big part of what makes them dynamic and creative. That is the point, as everyone there is looking for new ideas and viewpoints. You also do not want to work with people that are too pushy and tend to monopolize the group or with people that are too passive and do not contribute. The ideal participants in a Mastermind Alliance are Self-motivated, action-oriented and honest enough to do real work while also being capable of maintaining a healthy balance of exchange in social intercourse (as discussed in Lesson Six).

It is good for groups to have a moderator or facilitator and a few simple rules for maintaining decorum and helping to move the proceedings along. The moderator or facilitator does not have to be the same person at every meeting. The rules will vary according to the type of group, its size and the temperaments of the people involved. It is good to meet regularly and to keep track of time during meetings. These things reinforce the professional nature of the group and remind the participants that the group is not merely for socializing.

TAKING ACTION

1. Continue to evaluate and adjust your relationships and associations as described in

Lessons Two and Six. By now, most of your focus should be on seeking out and creating NEW relationships and associations with other people that have positive attitudes and beliefs about money and commerce.

2. In Lesson Seven, you were advised to consult with qualified professionals such as an accountant, an attorney, appropriate insurance agents and perhaps even an asset protection specialist as appropriate to your wealth-building needs. What progress have you made in this area? Have you assembled the professional team that best matches your situation and goals?

3. Go back through all of the main ideas and subjects presented in this course. In which areas do you think that a Mastermind Alliance would most benefit you in your wealth-building efforts?

4. Use the connective power of the internet to learn more about Mastermind groups and to find groups that fit your needs and goals. You can find lots of groups meeting either online or in-person in your local area by searching for websites that address the topics that interest you or by using a general resource like Meetup.Com.

5. Once you have some experience with Masterminds and other types of groups and have established relationships with other wealth-builders that you resonate with, consider forming

your own Mastermind Alliance that focuses on any more specific needs or goals that are not being addressed by other groups.

NOTES

NOTES

NOTES

NOTES

APPENDIX ONE: SETTING CLEAR AND ACHIEVABLE GOALS

To repeat a point made in Lesson Seven, long-term thinkers have a VISION of the life that they want and the things that they want to accomplish. Your goals provide a stable focus for your values and efforts so that your investments of time and energy result in productive ends.

This demands that your goals be very clear. While you can not pre-program every detail of your journey and its fulfillment - and should not try to - you do want to be very clear on what you actually want. There are some rules that help in setting clear and achievable goals, or in formulating what are called "well-formed outcomes" in Neuro-Linguistic Programming.

1. State your outcome in positive terms. Describe what you want, not what you do not want. For example, if there is something that you consider a problem, do not focus on not having the problem. Focus on what would be occurring if the problem did not exist. Focus on what you want to see occurring.

2. As appropriate to the operation, define the specific context, situation, relationships or environment needed for your outcome to occur. What, Who, Where, When and How? And Why? The more specifically that you define your outcome, the better that you can manifest it. Being specific tells you exactly what you should be seeing and makes success testable and measureable.

3. As appropriate, put yourself into the actions and experiences that you have determined above. Describe your experience in sensory-based language. What do you see, hear and feel? What exactly are you doing or saying? Focus on the rewards of your manifested outcome. Use your feelings of satisfaction from this picture as a motivator throughout the process of fulfillment (perhaps making a drawing or collage that represents the outcome).

4. Check for internal congruence. Does this outcome conflict with any of your other goals or values? Does any part of you disagree with or resist this outcome? Consider the activities involved in producing this outcome. How do you feel about them? Passionate and excited, or otherwise? If necessary, determine what needs changing and the personal work needed.

5. Is this outcome what you really want or is it a

mask for or means to a deeper desire? If so, start this process again with that deeper desire. Finally, specify the criteria for fulfillment. In addition to all of the previous criteria, how will you know when your outcome is well and fully accomplished? What specific evidence do you require?

6. Do not allow yourself to become overwhelmed by a big goal. If you have such a goal, break it down into its basic components and into sequences of doable steps. If necessary, mentally put yourself into the future where your well-formed outcome has been manifested and look backward to determine what the necessary tasks are or to determine what you need to research in forming a plan of action. When you have formulated the path, walk it. Take daily action. There is a saying that is applicable here: "How do you eat an elephant? One bite at a time." Use the game approach and stay in touch with your passion to keep motivated.

7. Use all of the resources and the bootstrapping process described at the end of Lesson Three.

You can use this process to set goals or formulate outcomes for all aspects of your wealth-building and world-building endeavors.

APPENDIX TWO: RESOURCES FOR FURTHER STUDY

The following works have much to offer in continuing your wealth-building and world-building education and endeavors.

ECONOMIC UNDERSTANDING

LESSONS FOR THE YOUNG ECONOMIST by Robert P. Murphy

ESSENTIALS OF ECONOMICS by Faustino Ballve

WEALTH PSYCHOLOGY

SECRETS OF THE MILLIONAIRE MIND by T. Harv Eker

THINK AND GROW RICH by Napoleon Hill

THE LUCK FACTOR by Richard Wiseman

PERSONAL FINANCE TOOLS

UNCOMMON CENTS by Lynn G. Robbins, Lisa Vermillion and Dennis Webb

START LATE, FINISH RICH by David Bach

I WILL TEACH YOU TO BE RICH by Ramit Sethi

KILLING SACRED COWS by Garrett B. Gunderson (exceptions to the rules)

MEET & GROW RICH by Joe Vitale and Bill Hibbler (on Mastermind groups)

WEALTH PROTECTION by Christopher R. Jarvis & David B. Mandell

RIGHT LIVELIHOOD

WISHCRAFT by Barbara Sher

THE $100 STARTUP by Chris Guillebeau

THE 4-HOUR WORKWEEK by Timothy Ferriss

HOW TO BE RICH by J. Paul Getty

MULTIPLE STREAMS OF INCOME by Robert G. Allen